Survival Communication:

Best Strategies to Keep In Touch With Your Family
During The Disaster

Table of Contents

Survival Communication: 1

Best Strategies to Keep In Touch With Your Family During The Disaster..
1

Introduction 3

Chapter 1 – Form the Plan 5

Chapter 2 – The Options 9

Chapter 3 – Radio 101: Your Options..13

Chapter 4 – Your Survival Checklist 18

Chapter 5 – Survival Communication: Making It Happen 20

Conclusion 23

Introduction

If you have any kind of interest in science fiction movies, you have likely seen movies at some point in which the power is knocked out. Whether it is some villain, aliens, or some huge natural disaster that nobody knew was coming, the power is suddenly gone and there is no way to turn it back on.

Which, in the movies, you see the characters make it through by using all sorts of things to survive, whether they are taking things apart, working devices so they work in ways you never knew they could, or if they are managing to get into the cell towers and turn things back on.

But, that is Hollywood, and Hollywood lets things happen that you wouldn't be able to do in the real world, and as a result, you would be left in a lot of trouble if that were to happen to you.

You see, in the world in which we live, we all like to watch those kinds of things, or we like to fantasize about them, but when it comes down to it, we wouldn't be able to do half of what they are able to do if we were put in the same situation.

Why?

Because we don't prepare. People go through life thinking that nothing like this is ever going to happen to them, and as a result, they aren't prepared when it does. You don't want to be one of those people. You want to be able to know with confidence that your family would not only be all right, but that they would be able to stay in touch in a situation like that.

That is why you have come to the right place with this book. In it, you are going to find what you need to stay in touch with those you love, no matter what happens in the outside world. You could end up lost in the wilderness, you could be the victim of a major natural disaster, or you could suddenly find yourself without power for another reason, and when that happens, you are going to be prepared.

This book is exactly what you need to make that happen, and by the time you reach the end, you are truly going to be prepared for anything life throws your way, whether the power is on or not.

So are you ready?

Staying in touch has never been easier.

Chapter 1 – Form the Plan

There is a huge reason why those around you call natural disasters or things along those lines "accidents". The reason for this is simple: nobody expects them to happen, and more often than not, no one is ready for them when they do.

We as a people have set up our towers and our computers to run quickly, to be in contact with those around, and to be available, but what we haven't done is set up a backup plan. Sure, you can depend on the old PC to come through if you need it to, but that is more the internet you are relying on.

When you stop to think about it, what is the backup plan for the internet? What is your go-to plan when the internet is down, or when the cell service isn't where you thought it was going to be?

You may think that if you are lost in the woods you can find a high place to call for help, if you can just manage to get a cell signal, even for a second, but what are you going to do if you try to call out for help, and you realize the cell service is just down?

There's nothing behind it, and there's nothing that can help you if you were only using that as your source of communication.

"Oh, that's not going to happen to me, we have tons of service and we live in one of the biggest service areas there is."

"Cell towers are numerous, surely if one of them is down, it won't be long before they are able to get another one up and running, and that only takes a few hours at most, then everything is going to go back to normal."

"If my cell goes out, I can always get on my laptop and write to everyone and tell them what is going on, that way I can stay in contact with them even with the towers down."

You may have though one or all of these before, and they are good plans to have, unless there is a major breakdown of power all at once. You may not think that could happen where you are, but consider this:

Tsunamis, tornadoes, earthquakes, flash floods, volcanoes, high winds... you name it. These are all very real threats that nobody has any control over, and though we can do what we can to keep them from affecting our communication, there are still going to be times when they break through our protection and disrupt what we are able to do.

Imagine your town is devastated by a huge earthquake. Imagine this is one of the largest earthquakes in the history of mankind, and it takes out all the power in the state, and you have no idea where your loved ones are. This changes your ability to just grab your computer and try to get a hold of them, because all electronic devices are limited to the service they're able to connect to.

Or, another situation, imagine if the United States were to be under attack from another country, and they managed to shut off the power. Sounds far fetched now, but if you really think about it, the technology that is available to everyone these days doesn't make that an impossibility.

So, you are going to need a way to communicate with those around you without the aid of cell towers or the internet alike. Both of these things are going to be off the table, so you will need to know how to stay in touch if this happens. It may be unlikely, it may not sound like anything you have to worry about, but trust me, if it does happen, you are going to want to be ready for it immediately.

I know you want to get down into the nitty gritty of communication in survival, but the very first thing you need to do is make sure everyone in your household is on the same page.

You can extend this to your neighbors, the people on your block, or even your entire neighborhood. Some have gone so far as to get their entire community on the same page. While this may not be something you have to worry about, the more people you can get involved, the easier it is going to be when it does happen.

In other words, don't be afraid to put together meetings, to hand out fliers, or to just talk about it with the people you are close to. Just like you want to have an immediate plan in the event of a house fire, you need to have another plan if you are going to pull this off large scale.

Most people don't mind listening to the ideas you have, so feel free to spread them. I am going to show you the things you can do to stay in touch with those around you in a crises, but you can take the next step and decide what you want to use, apply, and organize. Then, get your entire community on board, and you will be set no matter what comes your way.

Chapter 2 – The Options

I know I have already said that there aren't going to be a lot of help coming out of the computers or the cell phones, but I wanted to give you a rough idea of the ways you can communicate with those around you, so you have a list to choose from right off.

The things that you find on this list are basic, and I am going to pursue many of them later on in this book, but for now, I want to focus on the things you can do to keep everyone in contact no matter what happens.

- **Old school methods** – think smoke signals and morse code. These may be old, outdated, and things that you would feel downright silly doing, but if you are in a survival situation, you don't care about how silly you look doing something, if it means the difference of life and death, you aren't going to stop at anything.

  Either learn and teach those around you the actual codes, or come up with your own sets of signals to use, and you will have a direct way of contact whether you opt to use real fire, a flashlight, a whistle, or anything else you can shine or make some rhythmic noise with.

- **Passing messages methods** – while this form is hit and miss, unless you have a specific schedule set up, it is still effective. You can write letters that you leave or post in certain places, then you come back for later on to hear the reply.

As I said, this can be hit and miss if you aren't sure who is going to be where, when, but if you do set up a schedule of when you are going to drop off and pick up the notes with those around you, you can have a direct line of communication with the community, even if it is slow.

- **The fallback resources** – now all of the options listed up above are slow, somewhat unreliable, and limited to the range of hearing and vision you are dealing with.

In some, even many situations that could sneak up on you, these are methods that you will find to be effective in a variety of ways, but there are going to be times when you want something that is a little more reliable, not to mention further reaching.

When it comes to these kinds of things, what you need to focus on are radios. That's right, the old school, run of the mill radios with their many capabilities are able to provide a direct line of communication with the outside world, and others within the world you are living.

You can find radios that run off of solar power, you can get radios that are battery powered, and you can get radios that have incredibly long ranges, making communication across entire areas something not only feasible but easily accomplished.

In addition to these smaller radios, there are larger radios that can connect to mainstream devices, making you able to listen in on what is going on in the world as a whole, letting you know when and where help is, and letting you know what your next move should be.

In addition to that, it gives you a method to call out for help, to call for others if you want to set up a place to safety, and to spread your own news of what is going on in your neck of the woods. These radios are relatively easy to come by, and anyone can use them with a bit of no how.

With these in mind, you can see that there really is no excuse for you to not be able to stay in contact with those you love when the power is out. Sure, you can take these out into the woods, even using the flashlight or smoke signal methods, to communicate when you are out in the wilderness.

No matter how you decide to go about it, you need to pick the method you want to use, and get the rest of your clan on board. Make sure everyone knows what is going on, the language that is going to be used in that situation, and how and where to get these things.

Set them up in specific locations, and have everyone individually memorize where these locations are. If you are working with younger children especially, make sure each and every one of them knows what to do and where to go. This may not seem like that big of a deal now, but you never know if you are going to be in a situation where you are all together, or if you are all going to be separated and have to find your way alone.

Either way, get this set up right now, before anything happens, because these kinds of situations tend to arise without you knowing they are coming, and you don't want to put off today something that could potentially keep you all together tomorrow.

Chapter 3 – Radio 101: Your Options

If you show any interest at all in radios, you are going to find a lot of people that have their own opinions on what you should use. While these are well intended pieces of advice, you have to realize what may seem like a good idea for them may not be what you need for you, and you want to make sure you are getting what is going to work for you and your family.

Survival isn't a universal shoe, and you need to find the one that is going to work for you before you jump in and get down to it. So with that in mind, let's get down to your options, and figure out the best one for you and your family.

When it comes to radios, you are going to have your pick of the lot. There are some that are incredibly high tech and have tons of features, and there are others that are as simple as they come. I recommend you have more than one kind, and make sure everyone knows how to handle each one.

Find which one works best for your family, and you are set.

Two way radios or walkie talkies?

Your first impulse may be to head out to the electronic store down the road and grab a few walkie talkies... while this certainly isn't a bad idea, I would recommend you actually invest in a two way radio.

Two way radios and walkie talkies are basically the same thing, except you are going to have more features with a two way radio.

To say this another way, if you have a walkie talkie, you are going to be able to walk around and use it... hence the name, but this may not be the case with a two way radio. A two way radio may be handheld, and you might be able to take it with you, but that's not always the case. There are plenty of two way radios that mount onto vehicles or say indoors.

What's the difference between a two way radio and other radios?

The concept of radios can get confusing really fast if you don't know what you want. There are plenty of radios that are only one way... meaning you can hear what is being said, but you can't reply, or communicate with those around you. these are good for instances when you want to keep up on what is current, and for when you want to know the big news events that are happening.

One way radios are also more likely to have to stay put in either a car or be mounted in a house. This makes them a lot less portable, and more likely to get in the way. If you are going to want mobility, a one way radio may not be the best option for you.

With that in mind, a two way radio is going to likely be a better option as you will be able to take it with you as you move around

You never know the situation you are going to be in, and you may not be able to stay in one place for one reason or another. If you are going to be moving around, a two way radio is going to be able to follow you where you go. As you saw in the previous point, you may not always have portable two way radios, so you will want to intentionally purchase one that is small, and easy to fit in a variety of places.

This also raises the question of charging. Regardless of the radio you choose, it is going to run off of power in some way, so you will need to figure out how you are going to make this happen.

Thankfully, there are a lot of options that come onto the scene when you are deciding on the kind of radio you want to have. I personally recommend that you choose radios that can be charged with either solar power or physically charged. You are going to find that there are plenty of radios that you can charge through pumping them up.

The benefits to these radios is that you can charge them up at any time. There's no worry that your batteries are our, or that the battery didn't hold its charge in between the time you charged it and the time you needed it. Of course, your other option is to use solar powered batteries, which are also easy to find in a survival store.

No matter what happens, you are going to be hard pressed to not have access to the sun, so keep a pack of those in your box for any time you may need it.

You can feel free to mix and match the radios you use, and keep several on hand for a variety of purposes and situations.

When you are preparing for natural disasters, you want to be ready for anything that comes up. It can be hard to know what is going to come up, so with that in mind, you will want to prepare for things that could happen as well as the specific things that will happen.

What I mean by this is that you know the power is going to be out, so you need to have the supplies needed to get power to your radios, but you may not know why the power is out.

If you are in a city that has been torn apart by some sort of natural disaster, you will want to have a kind of radio that allows you to hear the news of what is going on.

These are good to have either in your vehicle or your safety zone, so you are always going to know that is safe. On the other hand, you are going to want to have radios on hand for everyone to take, so you know you are going to have communication with everyone no matter where they are.

Odds are, in this kind of situation, you are going to have people all over the place, so you will want to have them in contact with you the entire time. If you have both of these radios on hand, you are going to be prepared for anything that comes your way.

Chapter 4 – Your Survival Checklist

As I have already said, you need to have everyone on board as you prepare for natural disasters. To better prepare everyone, you need to have things to prepare them with.

For example, if everyone knows where everything is in the house, you can be sure they are going to find it if the power goes out. This is a lot better than the scenario of it being dark in the house and no one is able to find anything because they don't know where to look.

This can happen if you only toss things in your drawer or into a cupboard and leave them there. If you want to make sure everyone knows what to do and where to go, you never have to worry about searching for anyone, because they are going to do what they are supposed to do.

This is going to be a great peace of mind, depending on what happens.

With this in mind, here is your checklist to make sure everyone knows at all times.

- **Prepare your survival kit** – complete with enough radios for everyone, coats, bandages, batteries, etc.

- **Keep the survival kit accessible, and make sure everyone knows where to find it**

- **Keep your survival kit up to date** – if you have clothing inside, make sure everyone still fits in the pieces that are in there, and make sure nothing has gotten to the pieces (moths, mice, etc.)

- **Check to make sure your batteries are still charged, and that your radios are working**

Make sure everyone knows where this kit is, and how to find it.

Also have a safety spot in place so everyone knows where to head in the event of a disaster of some kind. This can be a corner of your yard, a nearby landmark, or any family place that everyone will remember.

Make sure everyone knows where this is, and review often to ensure everyone remembers.

You don't want to live life in fear, and you don't want to scare your younger kids by talking about things like this, but you do want to make sure everyone knows what to do in the case of an emergency.

You may have to assure them that nothing is wrong right now, but you do want them to know for a fact they can handle it if it does happen, and build up a confidence in them to go where you need them to in an emergency.

This is going to feel a lot better if you are ever in this kind of situation and need to know where everyone is.

Chapter 5 – Survival Communication: Making It Happen

The most important thing you need to know to prepare for this kind of situation is that staying calm is the only way this is going to work. If you panic, or if your loved ones panic, they are going to forget the things they need to make sure the radios work.

This is why I have reminded and encouraged you to keep practicing and making sure everyone is ready for this sort of thing if it happens. There is a real difference between being scared and losing your ability to focus, and you don't want the latter to happen. If you are going to see to it that your family members are safe, you have to make sure they know how to use things.

Don't just settle for using the owner's manual, have actual mock setups of what could happen, and practice. To do this, turn off all the power in the house, at night, so it is dark and there's no way to turn on the lights.

You can easily do this with the breaker, and with the flip of a switch you can show everyone what it is like to not have the ability to use the power. Make sure the computers are turned off as well as the cell phones, to get a real feel for what life without power is like.

This is going to show everyone, especially your younger kids, how to handle this kind of situation. Everyone, but especially younger children, are able to practice things better when they are in the situation itself, and that is better able to happen if you set it up that way.

This is why you see fire fighters train inside a burning building, or you see army men go into simulators so they know how to handle the real deal. I want you to find success in all of this, so set it up for how anything could be, and make sure everyone knows what to do and where to go.

I would also ask questions, set up scenarios, and ask what they would do for certain situations that arise.

I don't want you to scare anyone unnecessarily, but if you want them to know what to do, ask them what they would do if they were in that situation alone. Make sure they know what to do if they have to deal with an injury on themselves or someone else.

Make sure they know how to get a hold of emergency services, and what to do if those are down. Basically, no matter what could happen, ask them what they would do if it did happen, and you can rest easy knowing they are ready for anything that comes their way.

The more prepared your family is for this kind of situation, the better off all of you are going to be if it happens. Hand out the radios to everyone and show them how to use them. Show them how to find different frequencies and channels, and how to listen for answers or how to speak into it.

I recommend you have these mock trials at least a couple of times in a six month period, and that you reassure and encourage as you go along. The best thing you can do for your family in this time is to build up the confidence they need to know they are doing it right.

That confidence is what they are going to draw on in that situation if they are ever in it, and that is what will give you the assurance you will be able to communicate with them.

Conclusion

There you have it, everything you need to know to stay in touch with those around you in any kind of situation, using the things you have on hand. This book is going to change the way you view natural disasters, making you ready for anything the world throws your way.

It doesn't matter if you think you already know what to do when disaster strikes, it rings true that you can never be too prepared, and that is just what this book aims to do. I hope you were able to learn how to do anything you need to stay in touch with the people you love, no matter what kind of situation you find yourself in.

This book is going to show you just how you can make it through any form of trouble that heads your way, whether you are stuck in the wilderness for any amount of time, if you are without power in the town you live in, or if the disaster is further reaching than all of that.

This book aims to be helpful, and to get you to succeed. There's no way you can read this book and not come away from it without knowing what to do. The explanations are simple, the gear you need is readily available whether you go local or if you order it online, and the methods are easy to follow.

Anyone can do this, and the more people you get on board, the easier it is going to be to communicate with everyone if something happens. Going back to the movies you see, if they were able to have someone worked out so everyone would be able to communicate, a lot of the issues they face wouldn't exist.

So if you want to have the complete assurance that you are going to be ok in any kind of disaster, and that you will be able to communicate with the people you love no matter what happens, you are going to find what you need right here in this book.

Practice what you learn, form the plan and do the work in advance, and you are going to be ready for anything that heads your way, no matter what that happens to be.

It's so easy anyone can do it, and the results are real, so if you are ready to break out of the fear of not being able to communicate, and if you are ready to jump into the assurance that you would be able to stay in contact with those that you love or those that you need to in a disaster, you have come to the right place.

You are going to be a hero in that situation, for your friends, your family, and most of all, yourself.

FREE BonusReminder

If you have not grabbed it yet, please go ahead and download your special bonus report *"DIY Projects. 13 Useful & Easy To Make DIY Projects To Save Money & Improve Your Home!"*

SimplyClicktheButtonBelow

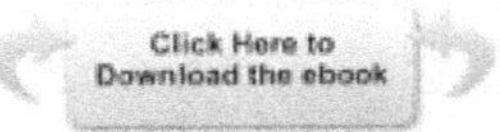

OR **Go to This Page**

http://preppersliving.com/free

BONUS #2: More Free & Discounted Books

Do you want to receive more Free & Discounted Books?

We have a mailing list where we send out our new Books when they go free or with a discount on Kindle. Click on the link below to sign up for Free & Discount Book Promotions.

=> Sign Up for Free & Discount Book Promotions <=

OR Go to this URL

http://zbit.ly/1WBb1Ek